APR 2014

Burly BULLDOGS

STRONG! STOUT! WRINKLY! PROUD! LOYAL! GENTLE!

ABDO Publishing Company

Katherine Hengel

Consulting Editor, Diane Craig, M.A./Reading Specialist

Published by ABDO Publishing Company
8000 West 78th Street, Edina, Minnesota 55439.

Copyright © 2011 by Abdo Consulting Group, Inc. International copyrights reserved in all countries. No part of this book may be reproduced in any form without written permission from the publisher. Super SandCastle™ is a trademark and logo of ABDO Publishing Company.
Printed in the United States of America,
North Mankato, Minnesota
052010
092010

 PRINTED ON RECYCLED PAPER

Editor: Liz Salzmann
Content Developer: Nancy Tuminelly
Cover and Interior Design and Production:
    Anders Hanson, Mighty Media
Illustrations: Bob Doucet
Photo Credits: Shutterstock

Library of Congress Cataloging-in-Publication Data
Hengel, Katherine.
 Burly bulldogs / by Katherine Hengel ; illustrated by Bob Doucet.
     p. cm. -- (Dog daze)
  ISBN 978-1-61613-376-4
 1. Bulldog--Juvenile literature. I. Doucet, Bob, ill. II. Title.
SF429.B85H46 2010
 636.72--dc22
                        2010001577

Super SandCastle™ books are created by a team of professional educators, reading specialists, and content developers around five essential components—phonemic awareness, phonics, vocabulary, text comprehension, and fluency—to assist young readers as they develop reading skills and strategies and increase their general knowledge. All books are written, reviewed, and leveled for guided reading, early reading intervention, and Accelerated Reader® programs for use in shared, guided, and independent reading and writing activities to support a balanced approach to literacy instruction.

CONTENTS

The Bulldog	3
Facial Features	4
Body Basics	5
Coat & Color	6
Health & Care	8
Exercise & Training	10
Attitude & Intelligence	12
Litters & Puppies	14
Buying a Bulldog	16
History of the Breed	18
Tails of Lore	20
Find the Bulldog	22
The Bulldog Quiz	23
Glossary	24

The BULLDOG

Known for their adorable wrinkles, bulldogs are kind and **loyal**. They are medium-sized dogs, but they love to sit on laps! They are also called English bulldogs. The bulldog's nickname is "sourmug!"

FACIAL FEATURES

Head
Bulldogs have large, round heads. They have short **muzzles** and flat foreheads.

Teeth and Mouth
Bulldogs have long, wrinkled **jowls**. Their teeth are large and strong.

Eyes
The eyes are set far away from the ears. They are dark and far apart.

Ears
A bulldog's ears are small and thin. They grow high on the dog's head.

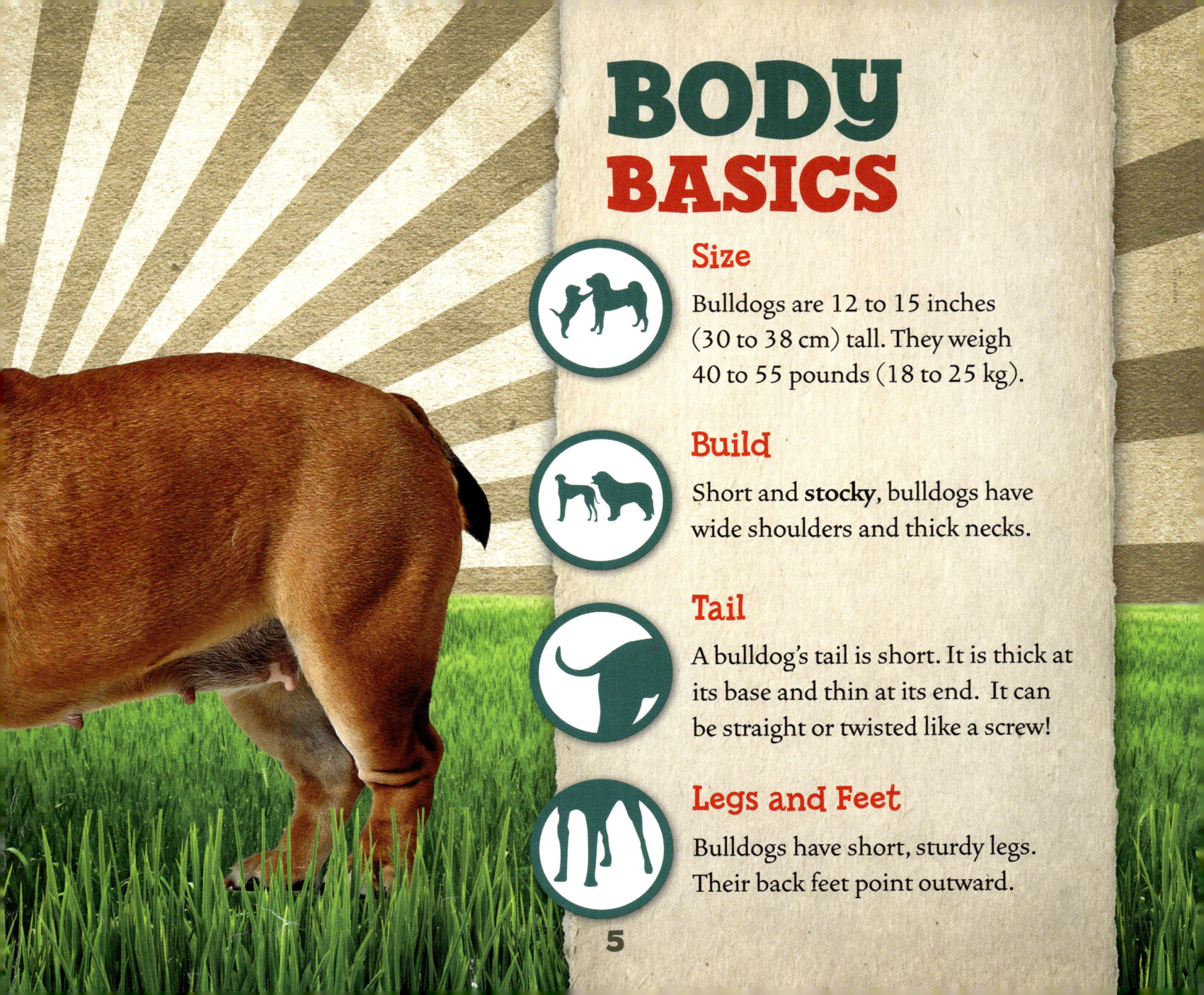

BODY BASICS

Size
Bulldogs are 12 to 15 inches (30 to 38 cm) tall. They weigh 40 to 55 pounds (18 to 25 kg).

Build
Short and **stocky**, bulldogs have wide shoulders and thick necks.

Tail
A bulldog's tail is short. It is thick at its base and thin at its end. It can be straight or twisted like a screw!

Legs and Feet
Bulldogs have short, sturdy legs. Their back feet point outward.

COAT & COLOR

Bulldog Fur

A bulldog's coat is straight, short, and fine. It is glossy and smooth. It covers all the wrinkles on the dog's head, neck, and shoulders!

Bulldogs can be several different colors. Some have **brindle** coats. Others are solid white, red, or fawn. Some bulldogs have piebald coats. Piebald coats are mostly white with brindle, red, fawn, or black patches.

RED FUR

BRINDLE COAT | RED AND WHITE COAT | FAWN AND WHITE COAT

HEALTH & CARE

Life Span

Most bulldogs live about 8 to 12 years.

Grooming

The wrinkles and folds around a bulldog's face should be cleaned every day. They can get infected, especially in hot weather. You may have to clean under the tail too.

VET'S CHECKLIST

- Have your bulldog spayed or neutered. This will prevent unwanted puppies.

- Visit a vet for regular checkups.

- Ask your vet about which foods are right for your bulldog.

- Clean your bulldog's teeth and ears once a week.

- Make sure your bulldog gets plenty of exercise.

- Trim your bulldog's nails about every six weeks.

EXERCISE & TRAINING

Activity Level

Bulldogs aren't very active. But they do need some exercise every day. Without it, they can become overweight. They don't like to walk much more than ½ mile (.8 km). Bulldogs are sensitive to heat. Never leave them in hot places. They can easily overheat!

Obedience

Bulldogs are not very **obedient** dogs! But they are excellent family pets because they love children. They are very gentle and protective of their owners. They can be **aggressive** toward strangers.

A Few Things You'll Need

A **leash** lets your bulldog know that you are the boss. With a leash, you can guide your dog where you want it to go. Most cities require that dogs be on leashes when they are outside.

A **collar** is a strap that goes around your bulldog's neck. You can attach a leash to the collar to take your dog on walks. You should also attach an **identification tag** with your home address. If your dog ever gets lost, people will know where it lives.

Toys keep your dog healthy and happy. Dogs like to chase and chew on them.

A **dog bed** will help your pet feel safe and comfortable at night.

ATTITUDE & INTELLIGENCE

Personality

Bulldogs are friendly and gentle. They love other dogs and people. They become very attached to their families. They usually won't leave the yard without them!

Intellect

Bulldogs are very kind and sweet, but like to do things their own way. Have you ever heard the saying, "stubborn as a bulldog"? Bulldogs can learn tricks, but they would rather be petted!

All About Me

Hi! My name is Bootsy. I'm a bulldog. I just wanted to let you know a few things about me. I made some lists below of things I like and dislike. Check them out!

Things I Like

- Spending time with my family
- Being outside when it isn't too hot
- Playing with kids
- Taking short walks
- Having my tummy rubbed

Things I Dislike

- Getting too hot
- Taking really long walks
- Being alone all day
- Having to learn a lot of tricks

LITTERS & PUPPIES

Litter Size

Female bulldogs usually give birth to four to six puppies.

Diet

Newborn pups drink their mother's milk. They can begin to eat soft puppy food when they are about five weeks old.

Growth

Bulldogs should stay with their mothers until they are eight weeks old. They reach their adult size when they are about two years old.

BUYING A BULLDOG

Choosing a Breeder

It's best to buy a puppy from a **breeder**, not a pet store. When you visit a dog breeder, ask to see the mother and father of the puppies. Make sure the parents are healthy, friendly, and well behaved.

Picking a Puppy

Choose a puppy that isn't too **aggressive** or too shy. If you crouch down, some of the puppies may want to play with you. One of them might be the right one for you!

Is It the Right Dog for You?

Buying a dog is a big decision. You'll want to make sure your new pet suits your lifestyle.

Get out a piece of paper. Draw a line down the middle.

Read the statements listed here. Each time you agree with a statement from the left column, make a mark on the left side of your paper. When you agree with a statement from the right column, make a mark on the right side of your paper.

I don't like being outside when it is really hot.	☐ ☐	I enjoy spending time in hot weather.
If my dog snores, that is okay!	☐ ☐	I want a dog that rarely snores.
I don't need a dog that likes to run with me.	☐ ☐	I want a dog that likes to run outside.
I want a dog that can get along with other animals.	☐ ☐	My dog doesn't have to like other animals.
I don't mind a little dog drool here and there.	☐ ☐	Dogs that drool are gross!
I want a dog that loves kids!	☐ ☐	It doesn't matter if my dog likes kids or not.
I want a dog that doesn't need a lot of exercise.	☐ ☐	I want a really active dog.

If you marked more X's on the left side than on the right side, a bulldog may be the right dog for you! If you have more X's on the right side of your paper, you might want to consider another breed.

History of the Breed
Brave Dogs from Great Britain

Bulldogs come from Great Britain. We can read about them in books from the 13th century! William Shakespeare wrote about bulldogs in his play *King Henry VI*.

Hundreds of years ago, bulldogs were taught to be **aggressive**. They were used to tease bulls! That's how they got their name. But bulldogs today are calm and lovable. They are great family pets because they are **loyal** and sweet.

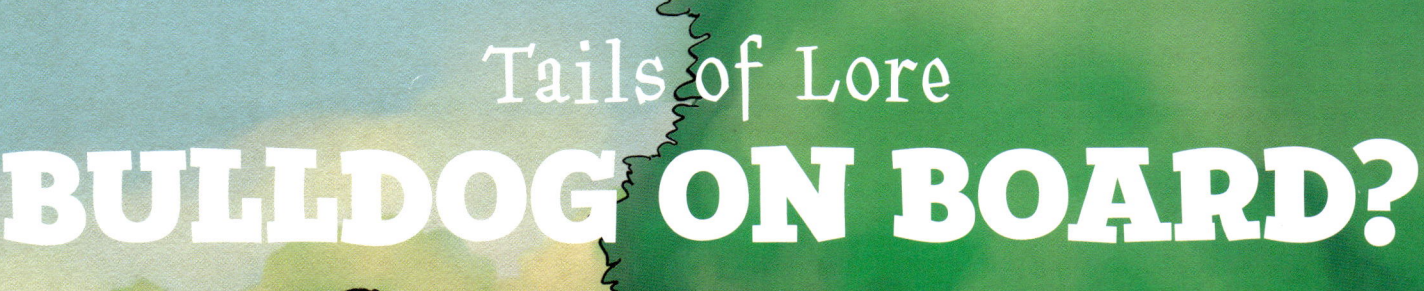

Tails of Lore
BULLDOG ON BOARD?

Bulldogs are known for the way they walk. They **shuffle** from side to side on their short legs! Most bulldogs don't like to go for really long walks. But that does not mean they are lazy!

Bulldogs are very alert. They love to do whatever their owners are doing! Bulldogs might walk funny, but they are very good at controlling their bodies. Some bulldogs will even skateboard! You should never force a bulldog to do this though. All bulldogs are different!

FIND THE BULLDOG

A **B** **C** **D**

Answers: A) Chinese crested B) Saint Bernard C) bulldog (correct) D) Dalmatian

THE BULLDOG QUIZ

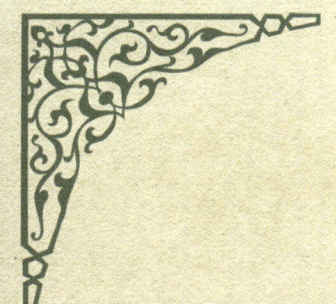

1. The bulldog's nickname is "sourmug." **True or false?**

2. Bulldogs have small, weak teeth. **True or false?**

3. Bulldogs have long legs. **True or false?**

4. There are no wrinkles on a bulldog. **True or false?**

5. Bulldogs are very **obedient**. **True or false?**

6. Bulldogs love people. **True or false?**

Answers: 1) true 2) false 3) false 4) false 5) false 6) true

GLOSSARY

aggressive – likely to attack or confront.

breed – 1. to raise animals that have certain traits. A *breeder* is someone whose job is to breed certain animals. 2. a group of animals with common ancestors.

brindle – a pattern with dark streaks or spots on a light background.

jowl – loose skin around the cheeks, throat, or jaws.

loyal – faithful or devoted to someone or something.

muzzle – an animal's nose and jaws.

obedient – likely to do as you are told.

shuffle – to walk without picking up one's feet very much.

stocky – short and thick.

About SUPER SANDCASTLE™

Bigger Books for Emerging Readers
Grades K–4

Created for library, classroom, and at-home use, Super SandCastle™ books support and engage young readers as they develop and build literacy skills and will increase their general knowledge about the world around them. Super SandCastle™ books are part of SandCastle™, the leading preK–3 imprint for emerging and beginning readers. Super SandCastle™ features a larger trim size for more reading fun.

Let Us Know

Super SandCastle™ would like to hear your stories about reading this book. What was your favorite page? Was there something hard that you needed help with? Share the ups and downs of learning to read. We want to hear from you! Send us an e-mail.

sandcastle@abdopublishing.com

Contact us for a complete list of SandCastle,™ Super SandCastle,™ and other nonfiction and fiction titles from ABDO Publishing Company.

www.abdopublishing.com • 8000 West 78th Street
Edina, MN 55439 • 800-800-1312 • 952-831-1632 fax